Also by MAXINE KUMIN

POETRY

Nurture

The Long Approach

Our Ground Time Here Will Be Brief

The Retrieval System

House, Bridge, Fountain, Gate

Up Country

The Nightmare Factory

The Privilege

Halfway

NOVELS

The Designated Heir

The Abduction

The Passions of Uxport

Through Dooms of Loves

SHORT STORIES

Why Can't We Live Together Like Civilized Human Beings?

ESSAYS

In Deep: Country Essays

To Make a Prairie: Essays on Poets, Poetry and Country Living

LOOKING FOR LUCK

W·W·NORTON & COMPANY·NEW YORK·LONDON

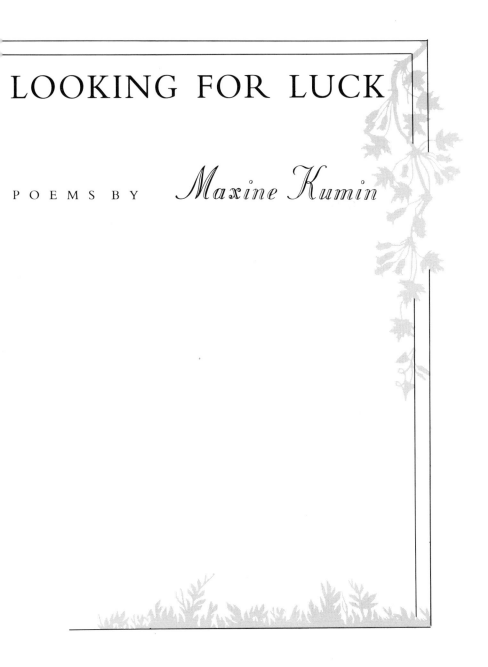

LOOKING FOR LUCK

POEMS BY *Maxine Kumin*

The text of this book is composed in 11/14 Bembo,
with the display set in Bembo.
Composition by Com Com, Inc.
Manufacturing by Courier Companies, Inc.
Book design by Antonina Krass.

First Edition.

Library of Congress Cataloging-in-Publication Data
Kumin, Maxine, 1925–
Looking for luck : poems / Maxine Kumin.
p.   cm.
I. Title.
PS3521.U638L58   1992
811'.54—dc20   91-20735
ISBN 0-393-03085-7
W.W. Norton & Company, Inc., 500 Fifth Avenue, New York, N.Y. 10110
W.W. Norton & Company, Ltd., 10 Coptic Street, London WC1A 1PU

1   2   3   4   5   6   7   8   9   0

For Yann and Noah, lucky cousins

CONTENTS

THREE

Some of the poems in this book were previously published as follows:

American Poetry Review: "Anniversary," "The Chambermaids in the Marriott in Mid-morning," "Indian Summer," "The Succession," and "Hay"

Arete: "Subduing the Dream in Alaska"

The Atlantic: "The Nuns of Childhood: Two Views"

Beloit Poetry Journal: "The Porch Swing" and "On Visiting a Friend in Southern California"

Boston Review of the Arts: "Telling the Barn Swallow"

Country Journal: "The Confidantes"

Crab Creek Review: "Waking to Moonlight"

Georgia Review: "On Visiting Flannery O'Connor's Grave"

Kenyon Review: "The Green Well" and "FAT PETS ON"

Mississippi Valley Review: "Getting Around O'Hare" and "Voices from Kansas"

The New York Times: "Credo"

The New Yorker: "Looking for Luck in Bangkok" and "The Rendezvous"

Nimrod: "A Brief History of Passion" and "Of Wings"

Ohio State University Journal: "A Morning on the Hill"

Ploughshares: "Saga: Four Variations on the Sonnet"

Poetry: "Progress," "The Geographic Center," "Finding the One Brief Note," and "The Poets' Garden"

Special Report: "Falling Asleep to the Sound of Waves"

TriQuarterly: "Taking the Lambs to Market"

The Women's Review of Books: "Remarkable Women: An Apostrophe" and "Ars Poetica"

Yankee: "Praise Be"

PROLOGUE

O swallows, swallows, poems are not
The point. Finding again the world,
That is the point. Where loveliness
Adorns intelligible things
Because the mind's eye lit the sun.

Howard Nemerov

CREDO

I believe in magic. I believe in the rights
of animals to leap out of our skins
as recorded in the Kiowa legend:
Directly there was a bear where the boy had been

as I believe in the resurrected wake-robin,
first wet knob of trillium to knock
in April at the underside of earth's door
in central New Hampshire where bears are

though still denned up at that early greening.
I believe in living on grateful terms
with the earth, with the black crumbles
of ancient manure that sift through my fingers

when I topdress the garden for winter. I believe
in the wet strings of earthworms aroused out of season
and in the bear, asleep now in the rock cave
where my outermost pasture abuts the forest.

I cede him a swale of chokecherries in August.
I give the sow and her cub as much yardage
as they desire when our paths intersect
as does my horse shifting under me

respectful but not cowed by our encounter.
I believe in the gift of the horse, which is magic,

their deep fear-snorts in play when the wind comes up,
the ballet of nip and jostle, plunge and crow hop.

I trust them to run from me, necks arched in a full
swan's S, tails cocked up over their backs
like plumes on a Cavalier's hat. I trust them
to gallop back, skid to a stop, their nostrils

level with my mouth, asking for my human breath
that they may test its intent, taste the smell of it.
I believe in myself as their sanctuary
and the earth with its summer plumes of carrots,

its clamber of peas, beans, masses of tendrils
as mine. I believe in the acrobatics of boy
into bear, the grace of animals
in my keeping, the thrust to go on.

ONE

LOOKING FOR LUCK
IN BANGKOK

Often at markets I see
people standing in line
to walk under an elephant.
They count out a few coins,
then crouch to slip beneath
the wrinkly umbrella that smells
of dust and old age
and a thousand miracles.

They unfold on the other side
blessed with long life,
good luck, solace from grief,
unruly children, and certain
liver complaints.

Conspicuous Caucasian,
I stoop to take my turn.
The feet of my elephant are stout
as planted pines. His trunk completes
this honest structure,

this tractable, tusked,
and deeply creased
endangered shelter.

I squat in his aromatic shade
reminded of stale bedclothes,
my mother's pantry shelves
of cloves and vinegar,
as if there were no world of drought,
no parasites, no ivory poachers.
My good luck running in
as his runs out.

PROGRESS

Eventually John Bunyan's Pilgrim
slogging through Despond, pronounced *slew*
by us and by the British, *slou,*

attains his goal the way enough
ants can carry off an elephant
and time will mend a migraine, derived

from *megrim,* a sharp pain in half
the head, such as an Indian paint endured
in Jackson Hole years back, his jaw fractured

by a savage twist of the hackamore.
Turned out to starve to death—the law of the West—
he waded into a distant slough instead

and spent the summer sucking up pond grass.
Healed, he became a champion cutting horse.
The boggy hollow is dark and perilous,

sometimes language impedes, sometimes it helps.
"Observe moon in first phase." The professor drops
articles to be more easily

comprehended by his Japanese
students who say, "To you, Hiroshima
is death. To us, is *beisbol* team,

long life, Hiroshima Carp."
They thrive in sloughs, these golden fish.
Such luck they do not need it deep.

PRAISE BE

Eleven months, two weeks in the womb
and this one sticks a foreleg out
frail as a dowel quivering
in the unfamiliar air and then
the other leg, cocked at the knee
at first, then straightening
and here's the head, a big blind fish
thrashing inside its see-through sack
and for a moment the panting mare
desists, lies still as death.

I tear the caul, look into eyes
as innocent, as skittery
as minnows. Three heaves, the shoulders pass.
The hips emerge. Fluid as snakes
the hind legs trail out glistering.
The whole astonished filly, still
attached, draws breath and whinnies
a treble tremolo that leaps
in her mother who nickers a low-key response.

Let them prosper, the dams and their sucklings.
Let nothing inhibit their heedless growing.
Let them raise up on sturdy pasterns
and trot out in light summer rain
onto the long lazy unfenced fields
of heaven.

ARS POETICA:
A FOUND POEM

Whenever I caught him down in the stall, I'd approach.
At first he jumped up the instant he heard me slide
the bolt. Then I could get the door open while
he stayed lying down, and I'd go in on my hands
and knees and crawl over to him so that
I wouldn't appear so threatening. It took
six or eight months before I could simply walk in
and sit with him, but I needed that kind of trust.

I kept him on a long rein to encourage him
to stretch out his neck and back. I danced with him
over ten or fifteen acres of fields with a lot
of flowing from one transition to another.
What I've learned is how to take the indirect route.
That final day I felt I could have cut
the bridle off, he went so well on his own.

H A Y

Day One: Above the river I hear
the loud fields giving up their gold,
the giant scissors-clack of Ruddy and Ned's
antique machine laying the timothy
and brome in windrows to be tedded,
this fierce anthood that persists
in taking from and giving back to the land,
defying the chrome millennium
that has contempt for smallscale backbreak.

Three emeralds, these interlocked three fields
free-leased for the tending and brushing out,
tidied up every fall like a well-swept
thrifty kitchen, blackberry and sumac
held at bay, gray birch and popple
brought down, the wild cherry lopped,
and gloriously every March
the wide white satin stretch besmirched
with dripping cartloads of manure.

Day Two: Sun bakes the long lines dry.
Late afternoon clouds pile up to stir
the teased-up mass with a southerly breeze
and since the forecast's fair, Ruddy and Ned
relax, play-punch, kidding each other,
calling each other Shirley, a name neither
owns up to, although once Scots-common

enough in New England back when
their patched rig was a modern invention.

Their dogs, four littermates,
Nutmeg, Cinnamon, Allspice and Mace,
Chessies with gums as pink as rubber
erasers and pink-rimmed eyes,
flat irises you can't look into,
their dogs, companionable roughnecks
always riding in the backs of their pickups
or panting, lying under them for shade,
look benignly on their sweating labors.

Day Three: The old baler cobbled from
other parts, repaired last winter,
cussed at in the shed in finger-
splitting cold when rusted bolts
resisted naval jelly, Coca-Cola, and
had to be drilled out in gritty bits,
now thunking like a good eggbeater
kicks the four-foot cubes off
onto the stubble for the pickups

and aggie trucks—that's our three-quarter ton
Dodge '67, slant-six engine
on its third clutch, with a new tie rod,
absent one door handle and an
intermittent taillight—
we'll carry fifty-two bales at a time
if they're pitched up and set on right.

Grunters and haulers, all of us
in these late-August heroics.

Interlude: The summer I was eleven
I boarded on a dairy farm in Pennsylvania.
Mornings we rode the ponies bareback
up through eiderdowns of ground fog,
up through the strong-armed apple orchard
that snatched at us no matter how we ducked,
up to the cows' vasty pasture, hooting and calling
until they assembled in their secret order
and we escorted them down to the milking barn
where each one gravely entered her stanchion.
There was no pushing or shoving.
All was as solemn as Quaker Meeting.

My four were: Lily, Martha, Grace and May.
May had only three tits. I learned to say *tit*
as it is written here. I learned to spend
twenty minutes per cow and five more stripping,
which you do by dipping your fingers in milk
and then flattening the aforementioned tit
again and again between forefinger and thumb
as you slide down it in a firm and soothing motion.
If they don't trust you they won't let down.
They'll get mastitis and their agony will be
forever on your conscience. To this day
I could close my eyes and strip a cow correctly.

I came to love my black and white ladies.
I loved pressing my cheek against each flank

as I milked. I almost came to love cowflops,
crisp at the edges, smelly pancakes.
I got pinkeye that summer, they say
I caught it from the cows, I almost lost the eye.
Meanwhile, we had squirt fights, cow to cow.
We squirted the waiting kittens full.
We drank milk warm from the pail,
thirsty and thoughtless of the mystery
we drank from the cow's dark body,
then filed in for breakfast.

They put up hay loose there, the old way,
forking it into the loft from the wagon rack
while the sweaty horses snorted and switched off flies
and the littlest kids were commanded to trample it flat
in between loads until the entire bay
was alight with its radiant sun-dried manna. . . .
It was paradise up there with dusty sun motes
you could write your name in as they skirled and drifted down.
There were ropes we swung on and dropped from and shinnied up
and the smell of the place was heaven, hurling me back
to some unknown plateau, tears standing up in my eyes
and an ancient hunger in my throat, a hunger. . . .

Perhaps in the last great turn of the wheel
I was some sort of grazing animal.
Perhaps—trundling hay in my own barn
tonight and salivating from the sweetness—
I will be again. . . . When I read Neruda's
we are approaching a great and common tenderness
my mind startles and connects to this

all but obsolete small scene above the river
where unspectacular people secure
their bulky loads and drive away at dusk.

Allegiance to the land is tenderness.
The luck of two good cuttings in this climate.
Now clean down to the alders in the swale,
the fields begin an autumn flush of growth,
the steady work of setting roots, and then
as in a long exhale, go dormant.

A MORNING ON THE HILL

High summer. A fat man with a skidder
is driving across our farthest pasture
gouging the green sweetness that is home.
My heart is black with hate for him
and at the point where the hill sharply ascends
I hope out loud the bastard will roll over.

With a roar the ponderous apparatus wavers,
tilts, slithers and ultimately upends
but here the dream stutters and falls flat:
merely opening a window he crawls out
the fattest man in town, unscathed
except just now panic attacks his chest

and he goes down in my sight like a shot steer.
I am running in place on thick and gluey feet
toward his emergency, this great
bear of a man I have met many times before.
Behind me, the earth gashed black by his cleats.
Ahead, shrilling toward us down city streets

the tearing sounds of the rescue wagon.
Waking, I remember the way a friend's
husband died beside her in his sleep.
Her voice on the phone was calm but taut as rope
that morning: *Joe is dead. Do me a favor?*
Call 911 for me. I've forgotten the number.

 3 0

Of course I'll call them. I'll come too.
Nobody dead up here this morning, though
the fat man tried. Now a relentless sun
licks the far hill alight. Its red balloon
lifts over lush pastures as if nothing new
has happened. Indeed enough comes true.

THE GREEN WELL

June. 5 A.M. Before the sun retakes
its dips and humps, light rims the field
with an aura. Gnats form an ectoplasmic cloud
over the bruised bathtub, over the salt lick

hollowed out by tongues, like medieval stairs
petitioners' feet have worn, looking for truth.
I hold truth in a Nine Lives can twice
weekly for the cats, whose paws explore

the lips and sills of stalls so deftly that
they need never encounter the grounded dogs.
Today a newly dead red squirrel hugs
the top of the feed bin, recompense exact.

Thanks, Abra. Thank you, Cadabra, for
doing God's work—fledglings, field mice, shrews,
moles, baby rabbits—else why would He
have made so many? I bury what I deplore

in the manure pile, deep in that warm brown
digester to be flung next fall on the meadow,
then let myself down rung by rung into
the green well of losses, a kitchen midden

where the newly dead layer by layer
overtake the long and longer vanished. Gone

now to tankage my first saved starveling mare
and the filly we tore from her in the rain.

After the lethal phenobarb, the vet
exchanged my check for his handkerchief.
Nine live foals since and I'm still pocked with grief,
with how they lay on their sides, half dry, half wet . . .

Grief, Sir, is a species of idleness,
a line we treasured out of Bellow, my
suicided long-term friend and I.
All these years I've fought somehow to bless

her drinking in of the killer car exhaust
but a coal of anger sat and winked its live
orange eye undimmed in my chest
while the world buzzed gossiping in the hive.

That mare a dangerous runaway, her tongue
thickly scarred by wire. My friend too
fleeing her wolves, her voices those voodoo
doctors could not still nor save her from . . .

The cats clean themselves after the kill.
A hapless swallow lays another clutch
of eggs in the accessible nest. It does
not end with us, not yet, though end it will.

SAGA

1. Life Style

Invincible begetters, assorted Scutzes
have always lived hereabouts in the woods
trapping beaver or fox, poaching enough
deer to get by on. Winters, they barricade
their groundsills with spoiled hay, which can ignite
from a careless cigarette or chimney spark.
In the fifties, one family barely got out
when the place lit up like the Fair midway at dark.

The singular name of Scutz, it is thought, derives
from *skuft,* Middle Dutch for the nape one is strung up by.
Hangmen or hanged, they led the same snug lives
in an Old World loft adjoining the pigsty
as now, three generations tucked in two
rooms with color tv, in the New.

2. Leisure

The seldom-traveled dirt road by their door
is where, good days, the Scutzes take their ease.
It serves as living room, garage, *pissoir*
as well as barnyard. Hens scratch and rabbits doze
under cars jacked up on stumps of trees.

Someone produces a dozen bottles of beer.
Someone tacks a target to a tire
across the road and hoists it seductively
human-high. The Scutzes love to shoot.
Later, they line the empty bottles up.

The music of glassbreak gladdens them. The brute
sound of a bullet widening a rip
in rubber, the rifle kick, the powder smell
pure bliss. Deadeyes, the Scutzes lightly kill.

3. Shelter

Old doors slanted over packing crates
shelter the Scutzes' several frantic dogs
pinioned on six-foot chains they haven't been
loosed from since January of '91
when someone on skis crept up in snow fog
and undid all of their catches in the night.

Each of the Scutzes' dogs has a dish or plate
to eat from, usually overturned in the dirt.
What do they do for water? Pray for rain.
What do they do for warmth? Remember when
they lay in the litter together, a sweet
jumble of laundry, spotted and stained.

O we are smug in the face of the Scutzes, we
who stroll past their domain, its aromas of ripe decay,
its casual discards mottled with smut and pee.
What do we neighbors do? Look the other way.

 35

4. Self-fulfilling Prophecy

If Lonnie Scutz comes back, he's guaranteed
free room and board in the State's crowbar hotel.
His girlfriend Grace, a toddler at her heels
and in her arms a grubby ten-month jewel,
looks to be pregnant again, but not his seed.
It's rumored this one was sired by his dad.

Towheads with skyblue eyes, they'll go to school
now and then, struggle to learn to read
and write, forget to carry when they add,
be mocked, kept back or made to play the fool
and soon enough drop out. Their nimble code,
hit first or get hit, supplants the Golden Rule.

It all works out the way we knew it would.
They'll come to no good end, the Scutzes' kids.

TAKING THE LAMBS
TO MARKET

All due respect to the blood on his bandsaw,
table, hands and smock, Amos is an artist.

We bring him something living, breathed, furred
and meet it next in a bloodless sagittal section.

No matter how we may deplore his profession
all of us are eating, even Keats

who said, *If a Sparrow come before my Window*
I take part in its existence and pick
about the Gravel, but dined on mutton.

Amos, who custom cuts and double wraps
in white butcher paper whatever we named,
fed, scratched behind the ear, deserves our praise:

a decent man who blurs the line of sight
between our conscience and our appetite.

THE SUCCESSION

The old dog, who can no longer breast
the steps to claim his musky nest
at the foot of the bed, wherefrom his growls
long warned the puppy not to trespass

now at the foot of the staircase howls
a wolfcry wrung from loneliness,
denying himself the solace of
the sheepskin rug by the woodstove.

The young dog, whose athletic leap
has usurped the favored space,
starts up, trots down to his grounded chief
and licks both sides of his face.

They lie like littermates on the black
ram's curly dead broad back.

RECYCLING

The sloth, who moves so slowly
through the forest canopy
as to be tinted green
from algae rooted in
the hair shafts of his thatch
which also serves as home
to a self-effacing moth,

sometimes dines upside down.
Leaves are his provender.
Heavy in cellulose
and slowly worked upon
by good bacteria
they take a week or more
to ask to reappear,

at which propitious hour
the sloth slowly descends,
hangs from a low-slung limb,
scoops a hole in the dirt
with his spadelike hind feet
and defecates in it,

thereby awakening
the self-effacing moth
who flies down to his dung
and lays her thousand eggs.

What firstly fed the sloth
now feeds the larval young

who, later in their growth,
are sealed in tight cocoons
they will burst from as moths
and, once their wings are dry,
sail up to the canopy
to seek congenial sloths.

TWO

SUBDUING THE DREAM
IN ALASKA

at the Beaver Dome Correctional Facility

In the visiting poet's workshop
the assignment is to write down a dream.
The intent, before the week is out,
is to show how much a poem is like
a dream set straight, made rational.
A dream scrubbed up and sent to school.

The reedy boy, so withdrawn
day after day he never gets beyond
printing his name in the upper
lefthand corner, is in for rape.

The big man with the jolly laugh
and beer belly is serving time
for incest. Two swaggerers in orange
jumpsuits have records for assault

with a dangerous weapon, which here
translates as knife. An older man,
exposed to his shame as illiterate,
has ninety days for poaching a moose.

He whispers his dream. The poet takes
it down in a lightning scribble
that will be difficult to read back.
There are caribou and snowmobiles in it,

cascades of antlers and a washbucket
of blood upended on the snow.
They say they dream of their ancestors,
the Inuit villages of their great-uncles,
seals whelping their pups on the ice cap,
the sun disappearing at winter solstice,
the treasure of their happy childhood,
the gift of their first flensing knife.

But in truth each night the conqueror comes in.
At a gallop he rides them, building our highway,
scratching up earthworks, laying our pipeline,
uncorking the bottle and smiling betrayal.

ON VISITING FLANNERY
O'CONNOR'S GRAVE

Milledgeville, Ga., 1988

Blindingly trite, this calling on the dead,
half obeisance, half an appeasing *there
go I*. We were born in the same year,
her birthday the same day as my favorite brother's,
he too died young of a rare crippling disease. . . .
These self-inflating notions nag me as
I drive through primordial red-clay country
past Brer Rabbit's Pawnshop and Flea Market,
past Uncle Remus's Real Estate and Museum
where I am stuck forever to the Tar Baby
who sticks to the next and next, a circuit
that will carry me by day's end to Memory Hill,

but first, an historic detour just this side
of what the local intelligentsia
in fond self-deprecation call Mudville
to take the cart track up to Andalusia,
the family seat, a serene remove from town,
as in a good Victorian novel.

Here, from the first-floor bedroom window
even on those last dark days, she could see
her beloved peacocks pecking and fanning,
the tribe of philoprogenitive donkeys
ambling down to the farm pond in the meadow,
a grove of ancient pecan trees bending

to be picked. Not antebellum grand,
but commodious Andalusia, with real gardens
harrowed every spring with real manure,
so that it's touching but not surprising that
when Mary McCarthy remarked, years before,
she had come to think of the Eucharist as a symbol,
O'Connor, considerably put out
by lapsed Catholic rhetoric, flared,
"Well, if it's a symbol, to hell with it."

They're haying in the swale. Machinery clatters.
Wood's been cut and stacked. I could walk up
to the empty manse and peer in past a shutter. . . .
The last descendants of O'Connor's critters,
one unkempt little donkey and a hinny—
the casual offspring of a female jennet
and a Shetland stallion—canter across the turf.
They won't come up for carrots, keep
the distance they feel safe in. Fair enough.

In town I pass the college, all mannerly
red brick, held fast as in a spell.
That last-begotten donkey's mournful bray
trails me past dogwood, holly, silver bell. . . .
What can an outsider know, except
the shell of things? The ancestral home
wants painting. Surrounding it, the handsome
latticework brick wall has major gaps.
At the end of the tranquil road, Memory Hill
stands on a rise so slight I want to say

to hell with it. Below the cemetery
mild traffic punctuates crow-call.

Not as I'd pictured her, enthroned
on high, fiercely Promethean
with eagles, say, or lions on the headstone—
but the square, unlandscaped family plot
sans even a drooping willow seems right.
Aligned with her father, three great-aunts opposite,
space for the mother who outlives her yet,
Flannery lies unadorned except by name
who breathed in fire and fed us on the flame.

ON VISITING A FRIEND
IN SOUTHERN CALIFORNIA

From the messily fecund trees she rejoices in
that arc and droop across her rooftop,
my friend estimates her head count runs
a thousand avocadoes a season.
Lemons as casual as acorns scatter
on the pavement, and oh the loquats raining
and the stain of superfluous persimmons . . .

In the eyes of a New Englander
God appears here a forgetful sloven
rotund and careless with cotyledons,
strewing the land with seed as if in mid-yawn,
letting a little of every unplanned
good thing trickle from the Almighty hand . . .

But who could overlook her favorite,
an elm brought overland in 1898
as a hopeful twig, now grown into a massive
Midwestern exotic that has outlasted
the rush for gold, the freeway toxins,
surfboards, fast foods, lotus-eating?
It holds on with a taproot deep as
the hellfire sermons of John Wesley,
wrestling the devil in soil and water
to go down sin-free into the hereafter.

VOICES FROM KANSAS

The women of Wichita say they live in what
is casually known on both coasts as a flyover state.
The prairie wind here is constant in every season.
Sometimes it makes the sucking sound of ocean.
Sometimes it moans like an animal in heat.

In April, deliberate fires blacken great swatches
of cropland. Scarves of smoke darken the day
devouring briars and thistles and climbing vetches
before seedtime. Tractors draw threads to the edge of sky.
You learn to pull out and pass, say the Wichita women

whom distance has not flattened, who cruise at a cool
80 miles per hour toward the rolling-pin horizon
where oncoming headlights are visible more than a mile
away. Long hours at a stretch behind the wheel
they zoom up to Michigan to speak at a conference,

revisit a lover, drop in on old friends.
They will not be sequestered by space. Jo-El,
descended from Socialists, is saving the farm-
labor songs of her forebears, accompanied by dulcimer.
Lynn collects early photos of sodhouse homesteaders.

Mary Anne has got a sad history in her arms.
She is reconstructing her orphaned grandfather
in his sea of sheep, white blobs overspreading the plains,

 49

his whole Scottish clan, ten siblings carried off together
in December of 1918 by a wildfire flu.
This tear-stained boy in the woolly fold, custodian
of his flock and her life, shines piercingly through.
As the grassland is rooted, so too are the Wichita women.
No absence among them may go unmarked into sleep.
Like wind in the wheat, the boundary blurs but keeps.

FAT PETS ON

I am trying to make a palindrome
out of the stencil NO STEP AFT
as we sit on the tarmac in Geneva.
It says don't tread on me, at least
not on this tender lifting place
where ice glistens along the wing
like juice beading a slice of melon.
I toy with FAT PETS ON while the intercom
announces that takeoff is delayed.

Long ago, before plexiglass,
before terrorists, each time we parted
at the international gate we could
still touch fingers, talk across
the token lattice that divided
ARRIVAL from IN TRANSIT in
Boston, Brussels, Singapore.
Daughter, now at the boarding call
limbo sets in. One more farewell.

Eyes forward, we turn from each other
back the disciplined way we came.
You with your briefcase and U.N. pass,
I humbler than that, a visiting mother,
carried by moving steps to my plane
whose destination—after Zurich, where
I will transfer to a jumbo jet—

is to refuel in Abu Dhabi,
home of twenty refugees in orbit,
those intercepts whose costly black-market
papers are not in order. People who
cannot come in from place of origin
and steadfastly refuse to go back to.
Month after month they languish, locked inside
handsome airport hotels at Zaventem
in Brussels, Schipphol in Amsterdam,
in Belgrade, Copenhagen, Bucharest.
However deluxe, still it is house arrest.

They may dial room service, see
interminable movies in
a tongue they cannot comprehend,
roam the carpeted corridors
but keep to the assigned floor,
suffer a continuum of clean
sheets and nightmares in which, shackled,
they are returned to death squads
or twenty years in hardship prison.

Meanwhile, I ride the current
of time backward, FAT PETS ON,
suspended in a calm cocoon
with Nanny-brisk attendants
to pamper the paid-up overfed.
They bear hot towels, hard rolls, a ration
of double-rich Swiss chocolate
to all of us luck kissed and safely set
down at birth in a privileged nation.

OF WINGS

Angels have eagles' wings
Renaissance paintings
conferred on them
or is it eagles angels?
Each makes a big tempting
target but an angel
the instant it is felled
resurrects whereas an eagle
once shot soon grows cold.

Angels subsist on ambrosia.
Eagles mainly on fish.
It is rumored that an eagle
will uplift a newborn lamb
but six lbs. is as much as
it can fly with whereas angels
as stolid as ants or oxen
can team up to displace
many times their body mass.

While Rilke's radiant vision
in every elegy sustained
him, what Benjamin Franklin
thought of angels is not known
but he declared the eagle
a bird of bad moral
character and proposed

the wild turkey instead
for our national symbol.

Wild is not the same as free.
The turkey's inability
to soar puts it upon
the ceremonial table
every Thanksgiving
thereby sparing eagles
or angels, both of whom
on attaining great heights
endure intense cold. Eagles

scarce elsewhere although
common as seagulls
above the dump at Juneau
when basking on air
between voracious forays
as graceful as angels
are objects to admire
nevertheless and will be
as long as we let them fly

while glorious angels
draped in genderless glitter
unseen as the souls
they purport to carry
excite us to be better
than we are before
they take us wingless and unsure
far beyond eagles
to the lockup in the sky.

GETTING AROUND O'HARE

Thoughts in transit while reading Heaven: A History,
by Colleen McDannell and Bernhard Lang

You can pick them out of the crowd, these true believers
in ancient tweed jackets with leather elbow patches,
the women professors in suits with matching briefcases,
medievalists from the congress in Kalamazoo

who, along with the rest of us arriving at Concourse B,
must descend by precipitous escalator
and proceed under the tarmac where 747s
rev up for takeoff, to arrive at Concourse C.

Heaven, to visionaries like Gerardesca
in the thirteenth century, was a radiant
light-filled space, richly embellished.
A holy city with ramparts seen to

by God and peopled with bodiless
beings who achieved beatific union in
other than sexual postures. So it is less
than surprising to learn, while abroad in O'Hare,

transported by moving sidewalk under a ceiling
of multicolored sinuous neon tubes
that blaze and ebb as the traveler progresses,
71 percent of the Gallup Poll respondents

agree there's a heaven where those who have led good lives
are to be eternally rewarded. *Look down,*
says the automatic voice as you break the light beam,
look down. The walkway is ending.

FINDING THE ONE
BRIEF NOTE

I woke this morning from the uneasy
sleep of a stranger in strange bedsheets
to bogus cardinal, robin trill
off-key, boisterous fake
crow caws, and at intervals
sounds that suggested the air brakes
of huge semis flinging themselves downhill.

In Greensboro, mockingbird capital
of the South, en route to teach a class
in prosody, I meet Delia
encumbered with stopwatch,
graph paper and tape recorder,
capturing the mid-fall melodies
of flocks of year-round mockers.

On a campus hedged with chinaberry trees,
while I am saying poems, she collects
arpeggios, engine music
and vaguely flatted masterpieces.
Delia knows that something good will come
from storing up these plainly suited clones'
repertoires each weekday

and I too haltingly assay
our single-minded still imperfect song.
We eulogize autumn, we long
for a better world, we seek to deliver
a purer hemidemisemiquaver,
the one brief note that says we mean,
roughshod and winged, to last forever.

WAKING TO MOONLIGHT

Bigger than a rabbit, surely, but
which one is screaming, predator
or prey? Whatever creature
dies this way, what

ever so slowly eats it alive
at the mouth of its burrow and leaves
no trace, the dog prefers
not to find out.

He growls at my side.
His neck hairs rise
attentive to the terrible high C's
scratched across the moon tonight.

By day I see that no fur fell.
No throat was cut.
This was not murder in the underbrush
but Eros, dipped in the flaming vat of estrus.

Whether more heaven than hell
a moot point for the pair that couples
with such protracted yowls and hisses.

THE PATRIOT

Old World *Rattus*
of Norwegian extraction
and dark complexion
enters this poem
a naturalized American,
swims under water
a hundred yards,
slips through a hole
the size of a quarter
and drops fifty feet
onto concrete,
an unruffled bird.
Like the homeless
he lives on discards.
Like them he is
a fact of life in
the metropolis.
Whatever comes down
—bits of bagel,
pizza, sweet roll—
is his.

Shooting him
at the dump
used to be
an honorable sport
for Sunday

in the country.
Men from the mill
would get up from dinner,
take a six-pack
in the pickup,
perch on the hood
and squeeze the trigger
of the .22
whenever something stirred.
Maybe only the toe
of a bread wrapper.
Maybe a kill.
It was comical
the way he used to jump
before the dump
became a landfill.

The year they closed
it down, everyone
with a barn, a horse,
a couple of leghorns,
a scatter of grain
began to catch
sidelong flashes
of that red eye,
that hairless tail.
Poison is touchy.
You had to spy
out the hole.
You had to watch
where the earth

was scratched.
You set the bait.
You learned the patience
of a lover.
You had to bury
his sleek dead body
over and over.
Faithful, robust
Rattus norvegicus
comes back to ghost us
in subway and cellar.
Wherever our roots are
his nest is beside us.
His head in the pail,
our nocturnal zealot,
his teeth in the trough,
ubiquitous patriot,
nothing we leave him
is ever enough.

THE POETS' GARDEN

After the first revolution
the poets were busier than
cabbage moths in the garden.
They praised the new nation,
the rice paddies, the rumps of the peasants
raised skyward as they planted,
the new children who would grow up to be literate,
have electricity, running water,
almost enough to eat.
They praised the factories
that belonged to everyone,
the bolts of black cloth
and the shimmering orange tractors
that ran like heavy-footed dragons
over the earth.

After the counterrevolution
the poets were excommunicated.
They were farmed out as swineherds.
They cleaned privies.
They swept the aisles of factories.
They learned to make light bulbs and fertilizers
and little by little they mastered

the gray art of ambiguity.
Out of the long and complex grasses
of their feelings they learned
to plait meanings into metaphor.
It was heavy weather.

After the next revolution
it rained melancholy, it is still raining
in the poets' garden. But they are planting
and busy white moths flutter
at random along the orderly rows,
a trillion eggs in their ovipositors
waiting to hatch into green loopers
with fearsome jaws.

THE GEOGRAPHIC CENTER

In they come, the Harpy-like great flappers,
a pair of pileated woodpeckers.
Like us, a faithful couple.

The male announces their arrival
daily at 3 with his harsh crow-call
across the ash treetops. They stay

an hour or so to peck apart
the strangle-vines of bittersweet
we say we'll thin someday to save the tree.

Word has been bruited around the county
we put out 50 lbs. of birdseed weekly,
five of suet, sundry crusts and crumbs.

It's January. Two feet of snow protect
the straitened ground. Deer have leapt
my garden fence and eaten clean the row

of Brussels sprouts that drooped there, armless
sentries. A mild one-lane flow
of creatures, mostly coyotes, let us know

they're foraging all night, nose
to the wild turkey tracks that skitter
around the frozen pond's perimeter.

Today my chestnut horse stands on
the geographic center of the pond.
He was born here, seven winters

must have taught him that it's water
under, but instinct isn't everything.
Last summer he came in as if bee-stung

galloping from pasture to the barn
with a muzzle full of quills. Why would
a horse, you ask me, poke a porcupine,

out of bravado or foolishness?
In World War II, basic training,
Alabama, all July you carried

a 50 lb. pack however many
sweaty miles they marched you daily
—and why did you enlist?—

before the Harvard clique of physicists
found and shipped you with sealed orders
to Los Alamos, another of the soldier-

scientists who worshiped Oppenheimer.
Our generation packed its 50 lbs.
from Hiroshima to the Pentagon,

from Selma, Memphis, the seedy back way
out of a hotel dining room in L.A.,
and most vividly, the gorgeous riderless

horse in full regalia that we carry forward
prancing, stopping, its stirrups turned backward
bearing the empty Presidential boots.

We shoulder what this life has lots
of, prisoners of hope as set
in our own way as the woodpeckers

whose bright red crests and red mustaches
glint against the flourishing bittersweet
we say we should but never will rip out.

THREE

A BRIEF HISTORY
OF PASSION

In the spring of 1912
Katherine Mansfield and John
Middleton Murry become lovers.
Mrs. Frieda Weekley runs
off with her husband's student,
an upstart named D. H. Lawrence,
and Virginia Stephen announces
her betrothal to Leonard Woolf,

a little Jew. My parents
are getting ready to meet
at my mother's piano recital.
They clash and elope. Katherine
had been, an early teacher said,
*a surly sort of girl . . . whose
compositions were too prolific.
She put herself in too much.*

My mother was anxious
to put herself out, escape
a boily Germanic household,
trade her eleven siblings
for the red bricks of marriage.
She too was a surly sort of girl
mooning over the keyboard
for hours with Chopin's *Etudes.*

While Katherine is dying,
traveling to Paris in search
of a cure with a charlatan doctor
named Manoukhin, instead of
touring the provinces as half
a piano duo, my mother
has settled in. She is having
her fourth baby (me) just as

Rilke finishes the seventh
Duino elegy and sends
his mistress a telegram
to report this triumph. But
so mercurial is the Muse
that walking back to his lodgings
another begins in his head.
He is up half the night with it.

My father, a sound sleeper,
was never seized after midnight.
He was not given to nightmares
or revised expectations.
The fact of his fierce courtship,
the dash in a borrowed Pierce Arrow
to a Maryland Justice of Peace,
astonishes me with its boldness.

But the long summer of their marriage
that stealthily fastened the door
against invading children
was not without chills and fever.
The relapses, the remissions

were dotted with honeymoon cruises.
Exotic postcards ("Dear All")
dripped through the mail slot's pursed mouth.
Silent, surprised nonreaders
taken aback by their offspring's
revelations on paper,
now they are gone I enjoy
inserting my ardent parents
into these other lives
that swell, like prideful bullfrogs,
with passion and commitment.

In a little room in the firmament
contiguous to the giants
of literary history
who raged on all sides around them
those good stars, Mother and Father,
shine out at this safe distance
casting on me their small
cold beams of bemused approval.

TELLING THE BARN SWALLOW

Once in Scheveningen on the North Sea
a girl on a camp stool played her cello.
She played while the gulls on the boardwalk rails
sat like stuffed toys and five oystermen,
five stick figures, bent to the flats below
and she played till the sea put the sun out.

Today in New Hampshire I clean
woods strawberries, those sows' teats
we picked this morning under the yearling pines.
The sun is going down, the crows announce it.
Only the barn swallow continues to zigzag
between the cello's double-stops.
She comes with a mouthful of mosquitoes
for the budvase beaks of her nestlings
banked in the overhang.
It is the same old sloppy nest.
She keeps sieving the air for them.
They are her second setting this year.

I tell the bird this is my child
fierce now in the half light
at her harmonics. I tell the bird
how this cello has crossed and recrossed
the Atlantic in its coffin and next week
will cross it again, and forever.

In the Second World War, the one I remember,
the Dutch culled infiltrating Germans
out of the Underground by making
them pronounce the word Scheveningen.
Scheveningen! Now she will raise her children
in a language that rusts in my mouth,
in a language that locks up my jaw.

The berries, those sweetlings fatter
than a tongue's tip, bleed on my fingers.
My daughter plays Bartok to the arriving fireflies.
The swallow settles over her foursome.
I tell the bird to cover well her hatch.
I tell her that this hour
must outlast the pies and the jellies,
must stick in my head like a burdock bur.

THE NUNS OF CHILDHOOD:
TWO VIEWS

I.

O where are they now, your harridan nuns
who thumped on young heads with a metal thimble
and punished with rulers your upturned palms:

three smacks for failing in long division,
one more to instill the meaning of *humble*.
As the twig is bent, said your harridan nuns.

Once, a visiting bishop, serene
at the close of a Mass through which he had shambled,
smiled upon you with upturned palms.

"Because this is my feast day," he ended,
"you may all have a free afternoon." In the scramble
of whistles and cheers one harridan nun,

fiercest of all the parochial coven,
Sister Pascala, without preamble
raged, "I protest!" and rapping on palms

at random, had bodily to be restrained.
O God's perfect servant is kneeling on brambles
wherever they sent her, your harridan nun,
enthroned as a symbol with upturned palms.

2.

O where are they now, my darling nuns
whose heads were shaved under snowy wimples,
who rustled drily inside their gowns,

disciples of Oxydol, starch and bluing,
their backyard clothesline a pious example?
They have flapped out of sight, my darling nuns.

Seamless as fish, made all of one skin,
their language secret, these gentle vestals
were wedded to Christ inside their gowns.

O Mother Superior Rosarine
on whose lap the privileged visitor lolled
—I at age four with my darling nuns,

with Sister Elizabeth, Sister Ann,
am offered to Jesus, the Jewish child–
next-door, who worships your ample black gown,

your eyebrows, those thick mustachioed twins,
your rimless glasses, your ring of pale gold—
who can have stolen my darling nuns?
Who rustles drily inside my gown?

REMARKABLE WOMEN:
AN APOSTROPHE

Beatrix Potter, on the stout side, dressed
"in tweeds thick enough to stop a bullet"
woven from the wool of your own sheep,
looking back across those green fields in
your old age you said, *If I had been*
caught young enough I could have become
anything. I salute what you became

and you, Louisa May, on record claiming
I was born with a boy's spirit under my bib
and tucker, working to keep the clan afloat
that Bronson Alcott dreamily left drift,
inventions on a tribe, book after book.
Eight Cousins was my favorite, orphaned Rose
saved from invalidism by Uncle Alec . . .

and you, Helen Nearing, almost ninety, kneeling
to dig potatoes for a guest's lunch, confessing
I was twenty-six before I planted so much
as a radish. Oh, I was lily-handed,
square-knuckled, liver-spotted, laying up
the house you built with Scott stone by stone,
tending the sugarbush, the raised-bed garden,

I salute you all, I take you with me wherever
I go to fire me with your fevers.

THE CHAMBERMAIDS IN THE
MARRIOTT IN MID-MORNING

are having a sort of coffee klatch as they clean
calling across the corridors in their rich contraltos
while luffing fresh sheets in the flickering gloom
of the turgid passionate soaps they follow from room to room.

In Atlanta they are black, young, with eloquent eyes.
In Toledo white, middle-aged, wearing nurses' shoes.
In El Paso always in motion diminutive Chicanas
gesture and lift and trill in liquid Spanish.

Behind my "Do Not Disturb" sign I go wherever they go
sorely tried by their menfolk, their husbands, lovers or sons
who have jobs or have lost them, who drink and run around,
who total their cars and are maimed, or lie idle in traction.

The funerals, weddings and births, the quarrels, the fatal gunshots
happen again and again, inventively reenacted
except that the story is framed by ads and coming attractions,
except that what takes a week in real life took only minutes.

I think how static my life is with its careful speeches and classes
and how I admire the women who daily clean up my messes,
who are never done scrubbing with Rabelaisian vigor
through the Marriott's morning soaps up and down every corridor.

FALLING ASLEEP TO THE
SOUND OF WAVES

How it was in the womb when she walked
cooked laughed shook out laundry lay back
in the tub unable to see her own toes

how it was when we lay hard by the walls
of that sphere overhearing the faint call
of voices, dog yaps, the grind and flurry

of gears starting up big machinery.
Close packed in our dark float tank, how we rose
and fell like the sea, all of us émigrés

to be, bobbing eastwest, northsouth
with the bud of a thumb in our billion fish mouths.

NOAH, AT SIX MONTHS

While, this rainy summer of 1990
the swollen pond pushes past its spillway,
bean seeds rot in their rows and lilacs
bead up but drop their thousand
lavender nubs unopened,

one silvery baby named Noah
is almost sitting alone now.
He sucks his fingers like ten tarts.
Through drool and Bronx cheer
he crows, inventing speech.
A river of vowels starts,
broken here and there by the chance
rapids of new consonants.

We kindle a fire in the parlor stove.
The farmhouse steams with the smell
of damp wool recurling
its filaments, like family feeling.
Shall we say all this is Noah's marvelous work?
Today in the rain our world is cupped in his ark.

ANNIVERSARY

Midday at Truro we walk on the beach
tritely splendid in jeans and sweaters
remembering V-J Day when we became lovers,
picking through pebbles and shells for old glass
the sea has buffed back to a natural plush.

The same men are pinned to their bluefishing poles.
Someone is flying a spiral kite. It falls
to the sand in a clash of primary colors.
Someone else has attached two inflated owls
to the balusters of his private stairs

that ascend in giddy zigzags the bluff.
One owl faces north, one south. They inspect
the hook of Cape Cod, this dazzling bleached place
the rich survey from their redwood decks,
the plain world we footprint every October.

It is still in my pocket, the piece that you plucked,
the soft pocked sliver of deep blue glass.

THE CONFIDANTES

Dorothy Harbison, *aetat* 91,
stumps into the barn on her cane and my arm,
invites the filly to nuzzle her face,
her neck and shoulders, her snowdrift hair
and would very likely be standing there
still to be nibbled, never enough
for either of them, so sternly lovestruck
except an impatient middle-aged daughter
waits to carry her mother off.

> In Camden, Maine the liveryman
> at the end of town, a floridly grand
> entrepreneur, sends for Dorothy
> whenever he has a prospect at hand.
> She is nine or ten. Given a knee
> up she can ride any horse on the place.
> If the deal goes through, a 50¢ piece
> pops in her pocket, but Dorothy's pride
> soars like a dirigible, its ropes untied.

It was all horses then, she says,
combing the filly's mane with her fingers,
soothing and kneading with practiced hands
from throatlatch to sensitive poll to withers.
All horses. Heavenly. You understand.

It's the year of the Crash. I'm almost four.
My father is riding a horse for hire
in the manicured parkland at Valley Green.
When he clops into sight the trees take fire,
the sun claps hands, dust motes are becalmed.
They boost me up to his shifting throne—
Whoa, Ebony!—and I put my palms
flat on the twitching satin skin
that smells like old fruit, and memory begins.

Leaving, Dorothy Harbison
speaks to the foal in a lilting croon:
I'll never wash again, I swear.
I'll keep the smell of you in my hair.
and stumps out fiercely young on her cane.

THE PORCH SWING

We embarrass each other.
He tells the assemblage at dinner
that he is my much younger brother,
a teenager who lost his hair
early, this cinnamon-toasted
bald squinting barrel-chested
man ten years my senior
who resembles sidelong the square
shape of our progenitor

and I am his none
too secret mortification,
a writer, a species of liar
thinly disguising the whereabouts,
squabbles, sexual habits
of people we lived with, namely
those voices and mirrors, our family.

Old orphans, our three middle siblings
dead, we look death straight
in its porcelain teeth, daring it
to squeeze onto the porch swing
where we rock away half a century

past Pop's mustache, his cubeb cigarettes,
his cap and squire's cape for Sundays,
the taffeta swish of Mama's best dress,
the maiden aunts stained from grating beets,
lifeguards rowing the breakers at Cape May . . .

We bask once more in our private sun,
the known astonishments of what has been.

INDIAN SUMMER

I watch the last grasshoppers taxiing
like wingless aircraft down some eternal runway
and the goldfinches suited up in their olive drab
working the field's blown thistleheads for seeds.

I watch my brother entering sleep on his side
both hands like a child's caught between his thighs.
The sun picks up a peach tone on his skin.
A blond fuzz softens the pillars of his legs.

We have come back from burying a sister.
He is not given to my several panics.
When he drove too fast swerving across the clacking
lane dividers to take advantage of
an illusory gap in the highway's steady flow,
I gasped. He was oblivious to my terror.

I watch the pulse tick in his temple, this stranger
who sleeps amid the busywork of sorrow,
the drying up, the bursting, the migration
and I think of the house of our childhood, a big
baluster rubbed dark and smooth in the middle,
stubbed up against but holding.

EPILOGUE

THE RENDEZVOUS

How narrow the bear trail
through the forest,
one paw print following
the other in the manner
of good King Wenceslas
tagged by his faithful serf.

How, according to the legend,
a bear is able to feel shame
and if a woman meets a male bear
she should take off all her clothes,
thereby causing him
to run away.

How I meet a male bear.
How I am careful not
to insult him. I unbutton
my blouse. He takes out
his teeth. I slip off
my skirt. He turns
his back and works his way
out of his pelt,
which he casts to the ground
for a rug.

He smells of honey
and garlic. I am wet
with human fear. How
can he run away, unfurred?
How can I, without my clothes?

How we prepare a new legend.

NOTES

"Credo" I am indebted to N. Scott Momaday, whose retelling of the Indian legend in *The Ancient Child,* Doubleday, 1989, sparked this elaboration.

"Progress" Jarvis Thurston, who grew up in Jackson Hole, Wyoming, told me the cutting-horse story from his boyhood. Robert Weinberg and Eleanor Wilner provided the succeeding anecdotes from their year as visiting professors in Japan.

"Ars Poetica: A Found Poem" Adapted, with his permission, from the words of David O'Connor of Upperville, Virginia, an outstanding trainer and a world-class equestrian.

"A Morning on the Hill" For Frances (Penna) Drew.

"Recycling" The symbiotic relationship in this poem is drawn from an article by Michael Robinson, *Smithsonian,* "The Diversity of Tropical Ecosystems," March 1990.

"On Visiting Flannery O'Connor's Grave" My thanks to Elizabeth Evans, who conveyed me to Milledgeville, and to Flannery O'Connor's cousin, Louise Florencourt, who invited us to Andalusia.

"On Visiting a Friend in Southern California" For Jean Burden.

"Voices from Kansas" For Anita Skeen and the women of Wichita.

"FAT PETS ON" The expression "refugees in orbit" was apparently coined in Geneva, Switzerland, by Minja Yang of UNESCO.

"The Nuns of Childhood: Two Views" With thanks to Joseph Parisi, whose harsh parochial school memories evoked my nostalgic ones.

"Remarkable Women: An Apostrophe" The magpie in me has drawn on three disparate sources for this poem, from Timothy Foote's article on Potter in *Smithsonian,* "A Tale of Some Tails and the Story of Their Shy Creator," January 1989; Louisa May Alcott's own *Selected Letters,* Little Brown, 1987; and Donald McCaig's article in *Country Journal,* "Helen

Nearing: The Good Life Lived with America's Premier Homesteader,"
January/February 1990.

"The Rendezvous" Alec Wilkinson's absorbing article on the Tlingits of Ad-
miralty Island (*The New Yorker,* November 26, 1990) gave rise to this
poem.